NATIONAL GEOGRAPHIC

Vanishing Cultures

PIONEER EDITION

By Wade Davis

CONTENTS

Earth has at least 5,000 traditional cultures. But the world is changing. Can those age-old ways of life survive?

Vanishing

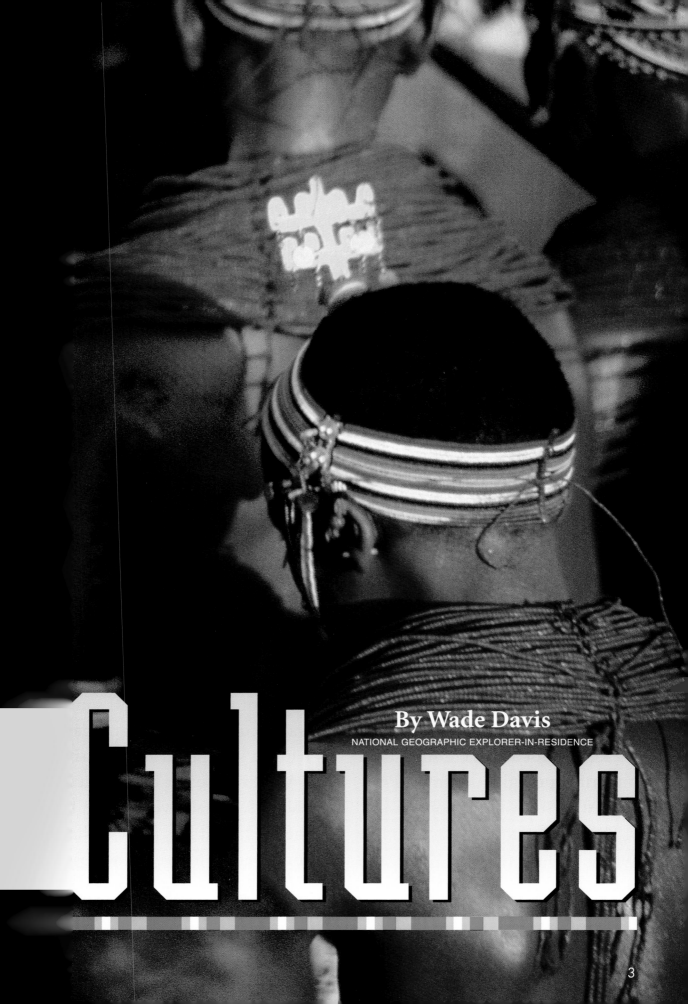

Cultures

By Wade Davis
NATIONAL GEOGRAPHIC EXPLORER-IN-RESIDENCE

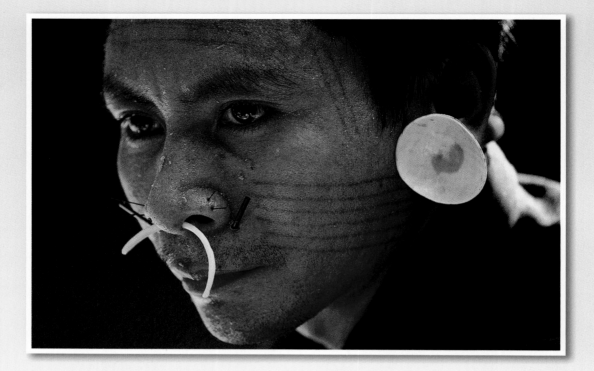

Tepi (above) was born about 25 years ago. He is part of the Matis tribe. They live in Brazil. When he was born, his tribe met outsiders for the first time. Everything changed. Tribe members gave up their old ways. But Tepi and a few others keep their customs alive.

The Matis are not alone. Many old **cultures** are disappearing. A culture is a group's way of life. It is their clothing and food. It is their music and much more.

I know a lot about cultures. I am an **anthropologist** (an thruh PAH luh jist). I study how people live.

The people I study live in faraway places. So I get to go on many trips. Sometimes I have to hike to villages. Once I spent ten days lost in a jungle. I have even eaten termites!

I am always learning about people. I discover how we are different. I also see how we are alike. It's a lot of fun!

Part of my job is hard. I sometimes watch cultures disappear. That can happen when their habitats shrink.

We do not often talk about human habitats. But all living things have them. Habitat loss makes it hard for some people to live as they used to.

Let's look at three vanishing cultures. To do so, we will go to Africa, Asia, and South America.

The Ariaal

Our first stop is Kenya. It is a country in Africa. Kenya is home to the Ariaal. About 10,000 people belong to the tribe.

The Ariaal live on grassland. They herd cattle and camels. They get much of their food from the animals.

The area is hot and dry. It is often hard to find enough water for all the animals.

That is why the Ariaal live as **nomads.** They move from place to place, looking for food and water.

When one spot gets too dry, the tribe moves. That worked for a long time. Then about 30 years ago, their lives changed.

Less rain started to fall. Wars broke out in nearby countries. Both the dry spell and wars started a **famine,** or food shortage. Some government officials wanted the tribe to settle down. They told the Ariaal to move into villages.

Many Ariaal did not give up their old ways. They moved to the slopes of nearby mountains. There they have been able to keep their culture.

Happy Voices. *Ariaal women sing as they head to a wedding.*

PAUL CHESLEY, NATIONAL GEOGRAPHIC IMAGE COLLECTION (PENAN); NG MAPS; NICOLAS REYNARD, NATIONAL GEOGRAPHIC IMAGE COLLECTION (MASK)

The Penan

Aiming to Survive. *A Penan hunter uses a blowpipe to shoot a poison dart at an animal. The Penan hunt monkeys, deer, and wild boars.*

Our next stop is Borneo. It is a Pacific Ocean island. Borneo is covered by rain forests. The island gets up to 210 inches of rain each year.

About 300 members of the Penan tribe live in the forest. I have spent a long time studying them.

The Penan are nomads. They find everything they need in their habitat.

They hunt wild pigs. They harvest fruit. They use vines to make string. They even make a special kind of flour from a palm tree.

The Penan share everything. Not sharing is one of the worst things a Penan can do.

Today some newcomers do not want to share with the Penan. They are cutting down large parts of the rain forest habitat.

More than 6,000 Penan have fled the shrinking jungle. They have moved into camps. Life in the camps is hard. Jobs are rare. The Penan no longer wear their traditional clothes. Their ancient culture is disappearing.

The Flecheiros

Brazil is our last stop. Much of the country is covered by rain forests. Some people want to cut down the forests.

The Flecheiros live in the forest. They are one of 17 tribes in Brazil that have never met outsiders.

Recently an official from Brazil went to look for the Flecheiros, or Arrow People. He did not want to meet them. He wanted to find where they live to help protect them. Local guides led him into the forest. One of them was Tepi (page 4).

Hiking along a path, the official saw something. Someone had placed a young tree across the path. It was a warning to stay away from the Arrow People's village. The team quickly changed direction.

Changing directions did not help. The team came upon a village anyway. The Arrow People live there. Luckily, they had just left the village. Their cooking fires were still warm.

Before leaving, the Arrow People were making a feast. They had piles of food—monkey and turtle meat.

Near the fires were masks made of tree bark. Clay pots held red dye. The Arrow People probably use the dye to color their faces and bodies.

We may never know what the feast was for. We cannot know how long the Arrow People can stay away from outsiders. We do know that they and many other people do not want to change. They want to keep their old ways. But will they be able to?

Mystery Man. *An explorer tries on a mask found in the Arrow People's village. We know little about their lives.*

Wordwise

anthropologist: scientist who studies human cultures

culture: how a group lives

famine: extreme food shortage

nomad: person who moves around

Vanishing Habitats

Modern life is changing many habitats around the world. These changes can affect the plants and animals in these habitats—and the people too.

RAIN FORESTS

Habitat Features A rain forest is a tree-filled area. It gets a lot of rain all year long. Many kinds of plants and animals live in rain forests.

Location Some rain forests stay warm all year. They are near the Equator. Others are in cooler areas near the coast.

Dangers Every year, people cut down more rain forests. They build new homes and roads. This destroys the homes of many rain forest plants and animals.

SAVANNAS

Habitat Features A savanna is a grassland area. It has few shrubs or trees. Many savannas are dry. Others flood sometimes.

Location Large savannas are found in Africa, Asia, and South America. Smaller ones are found in Australia and North America.

Dangers Floods are important to some savannas. Plants and animals depend on them. But people often put dams on rivers. This keeps them from flooding. It hurts savannas.

DESERTS

Habitat Features A desert is an area that gets very little rain. Most deserts are sandy or rocky. But some have snow and ice.

Location Every continent, even Antarctica, has desert land. Large deserts are found in Africa, Asia, and Australia.

Dangers People drive cars and off-road vehicles across deserts. This damages the desert soil. It causes trouble for a desert's plants and animals.

GLACIERS AND ICE SHEETS

Habitat Features A glacier is a mass of ice that moves over land. A glacier that covers more than 19,305 square miles is an ice sheet.

Location Glaciers are often found along mountain ranges. Earth has only two ice sheets. They are on Antarctica and Greenland.

Dangers Earth is getting warmer. Glaciers and ice sheets are slowly melting away. The ice becomes water when it melts. The water could flood some areas.

A World of Habitats

Use this map to locate different habitats around the world.

ARCTIC

Elk
© EYEWIRE IMAGES

NORTH AMERICA

Brown bear
GEORGE F. MOBLEY

NORTH PACIFIC OCEAN

Red fox
ROYALTY-FREE, CORBIS

NORTH ATLANTIC OCEAN

Raccoon
© EYEWIRE IMAGES

Keel-billed toucan
© DIGITAL VISION

Poison-dart frog
MARK W. MOFFETT

SOUTH AMERICA

Lowland
MICHAEL NICHOLS

Galápagos tortoise
© DIGITAL VISION

Humpback whale
FLIP NICKLIN

Lion

SOUTH PACIFIC OCEAN

Jaguar
TOM BRAKEFIELD, BRUCE COLEMAN, INC.

Golden lion tamarin
MICHAEL NICHOLS, NG IMAGE COLLECTION

Gentoo penguin
© DIGITAL VISION

A

PHOTODISC (LEAVES AND PINECONE); RICHARD OLSENIUS (TREES); NG MAPS (MAP).

Map Key

Rain Forest This damp world of tall trees and vines provides habitats for countless animals.

Hardwood Forest This habitat has trees with leaves that fall off each year.

Evergreen Forest This forest habitat has trees, such as pines and firs, with leaves that stay on all year.

Scrubland Scrubland is home to small trees and shrubs that can survive long, dry summers.

Prairie A prairie is like [a] sea of wild grasses. This habitat is also known [as] a steppe.

Savanna Warm and often [dry], a savanna is a mix of [grasses] and clumps of trees.

Desert Deserts get ten or fewer inches of rain a year. Cactuses survive here by storing water.

Highland This habitat is far above sea level. Winds are strong, and weather is cold.

Tundra Tundras are bitterly cold lands, mainly around the Arctic Ocean, with small plants.

Ice Sheets Ice sheets cover Antarctica and a large area of Greenland.

Cultures

Answer these questions to find out what you learned about cultures.

1 What is an anthropologist?

2 How does an anthropologist learn about cultures?

3 Why are some cultures struggling to survive?

4 What are habitats?

5 Why are some habitats in danger?